For Jana, for the blessings and love you show me every day.

-Sally

For my three beautiful children, Jordan, Billie and Zoë. Thank you for filling my life with colour, love, happiness and pure joy. And thank you Jordan for teaching us every day that love doesn't count chromosomes.

-Alexis

Every morning, when the sun was shining high in the sky,

Jana would wake up with a happy song, a big laugh,

and a fun game of hide-and-seek behind the curtains.

This time, she climbed out of bed and ran straight to her sock drawer.

"Mmm, which one?" She reached for the polka dot socks that had little ribbons that went all around her ankles.

Jana had just learned how to put on her socks all by herself. To celebrate, her mum and dad bought her heaps of incredible socks. She had a drawer full of them. They had all her favourite colours and shapes.

There was pink, purple, and lots of yellow, of course.

Some had stars and rainbows.

Others had butterflies, and some had pompoms.

Jane wore her new socks everywhere she went.

She wore them to the playground.

And she wore them when she went to school.

"Look, look," said Jana.

All her friends were very excited to see how good she was at putting her socks on. They cheered, clapped, and gave her high-fives.

Jana loved playing with her friends.
They took turns on the slide. "Weeeee!"

They ate their lunch together. "Yum-my!"

They raced, and her friends waited if Jana fell behind. They didn't mind that she didn't say as many words as they did. They loved Jana just as she was.

When her friends saw her marvellous socks, they all wanted a pair of brightly coloured socks, too.

"Hmmm..." Jana had an idea!

As she packed her backpack that morning, Jana put in an extra pair of socks for one of her friends.

She did this every single day until one day; there were none left! She had given all her socks away, but she was happy because everyone was having fun.

Jana's socks were so popular that, one day, Jana's teacher announced they would have a sock parade on the last day of school.

"What's a sock parade?"

"Everyone walks around showing off their brightest socks.
All the mummies and daddies will be there.
And, there's going to be a big surprise!"

On the day of the parade,
Jana pointed at all the socks
in their beautiful colours.

Jana and her friends ran to the far end of the schoolyard. Bubbles were floating up in the air, and there was a giant jumping castle.

"Look! There's something inside,"
said one of her friends.

In the middle of the jumping castle, there sat a giant box with a bright blue and yellow ribbon.

"It's for Jana! It has her name on it!"

All the children gathered around. There was her name, in big yellow glittery letters:

J.A.N.A.

"What's inside?" asked Jana looking at her friends with excitement.

"Open it, Jana," the children giggled.

"It's a puppy!"

"No, it's cake!"

"I think it's pizza with lots of cheese!"

The children giggled some more. Jana pulled at the ribbon with her fingers, and everyone gasped in delight as several yellow balloons sprung out of the box.

"Balloooons!"

There, hiding underneath the balloons, were dozens of brightly coloured socks.

"Socks! Socks!" Jana exclaimed.

"Jana, all these socks are for you."

"For me? For Jana?" asked Jana.

"Yes, for you, Jana! You were very kind. You shared your socks with all of your friends. Everyone wanted to give you this wonderful present."

Jana laughed and clapped her hands. "Yay! Hooray!"

"Thank you, Jana!" sang the children.

"Thank you," Jana sang back.

She gave each of her friends a big, squishy hug.

Then they threw all of the socks up in the air along with
balloons, confetti, and all things fun as they bounced
and bopped about on the jumping castle.

The brightly coloured socks flew everywhere.
And even though all of the socks were different,
they were all still the same thing – socks!

Jana may be a little different, too,
but she is still the same as everyone else.
And you know what?

It's okay to be a little different because that's what makes the world a fun, fantastic and brightly coloured place to be.

Lightning Source UK Ltd.
Milton Keynes UK
UKHW021055170922
409001UK00002B/109